By Pearl Grace Cornell

Illustrations by Ray D Schwab

Cover Photo Courtesy of Monica Bryant Photography
Colorado Springs, CO
www.monicabryantphotography.com

© 2008 by Pearl G Cornell
ISBN 978-0-9818403-0-7

Published by:
Pearls of Grace Publishing
1705 S 4 St; Broken Arrow, OK 74012
918-286-6130

All illustrations were drawn by Ray D Schwab
Broken Arrow, OK

Cover Photo Courtesy of Monica Bryant Photography
Colorado Springs, CO
www.monicabryantphotography.com

CONTENTS

iii

ACKNOWLEDGMENTS

Sincere appreciation goes to Sam and Sharon Osborn, who tirelessly and patiently walked me through setting up my document. Style and formatting were particularly difficult. Thanks to them, I still have some hair left on my head. Their expertise in this area was shared with me even at the midnight hour.

Larry Bishop encouraged, and push-started me down this journey.

Thanks to Ray Schwab for exemplifying my words with his creative drawings.

My grandchildren were supportive and reassuring all the way. Page 39 was included, at the suggestion of my grandson, Ryan Schwab.

Thank you, Mother for training and forming my childhood years. You embedded the Word of God into my mind as a child. God has been my source because of your teaching.

God molded me into who I am today. He was my primary guide and inspiration all the way through this book. Without the supervision of the sweet Holy Spirit, I would have given up the idea before completion. I can do all things through Christ who strengthens me.

A big "Oklahoma Thanks" to all of you.

INTRODUCTION

In writing this book, the dominating thought was to give sundry ways of looking at every day problems and struggles. Pointing others to Jesus is my number one goal because Jesus is the answer. He is the way, the truth, and the life. No man approaches the Father except through Him.

Hopefully the little aphorisms will uplift, encourage, strengthen and amuse you as you read through each section.

Try putting to memory the ones that meet your particular need. Recall them, as the need arises. In that way your life will become stronger, brighter, and happier. Then you can spread joy to your family and beyond. If anything needs healing, it is the 21st century family.

Our daily lives are filled with too much stress and discord. Jobs, traffic, and you name it, all cause stress in our lives. That stress is then transferred to the ones we really love the most, but don't show it. Parents, please make an effort to be happier so your family will stand firm. Our country will become stronger if we strengthen ourselves first.

Let God speak to you as you read. It was planned so you don't have to follow the usual order of glancing straight through. You can thumb through the pages and if something catches your eye stop there.

Pick it up when you have ten minutes to spare. Keeping a copy in your car may eliminate the fuming when you have to wait on your kids or spouse. You just might not be irritable when they arrive. It will make the waiting seem like seconds instead of minutes...minutes instead of an hour.

If this little book helps just one person, then the hours of preparation were worth it. Hopefully you will be that person.

My prayer is that God's Word and the Holy Spirit will have free course in your life, and that you be delivered from anything evil and wicked.

Pearl G Cornell

Section I

THE ALPHA

GOD'S

CARPENTER

IS BUILDING ME A

MANSION

Mark 6: 3 Is not this the carpenter, the son of Mary...
John 14:2 In my Father's house are many *mansions*: if it were not
so, I would have told you. I go to prepare a place for you.

A
WONDERFUL COUNSELOR IS CALLING

WILL YOU ANSWER ?

Isaiah 9: 6 For unto us a child is born, unto us a son is given: and the government shall be upon his shoulder: and his name shall be called *Wonderful, Counsellor*
*Isaiah 49 :*1 Listen to me, all of you in far-off lands! The Lord called me before my birth; from within the womb he called me by name. (NLT)

THE CARPENTER

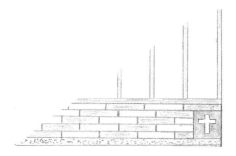

Mark 6: 3 Is not this the carpenter, the son of Mary
Ephesians 2: 20 We are his house, built on the foundation of the
apostles and the prophets. And the *cornerstone* is Christ Jesus
himself. (NLT)

WORDS OF THE

GREAT TEACHER

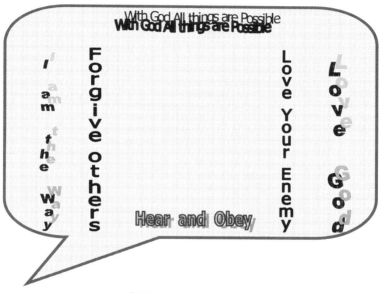

STILL TUTOR

John 3: 1, 2 There was a man of the Pharisees, named Nicodemus, a ruler of the Jews: The same came to Jesus by night, and said unto him, Rabbi, we know that thou art a teacher come from God:
Psalm 119: 98 Your commands make me wiser than my enemies, for your commands are my constant guide. (NLT)

Smell like the world

Bathe yourself in

the rose of Sharon

AND

the lily of the valley.

Song of Solomon 2: 1 "I am the rose of Sharon, and the lily of the valleys."

THE HOLY ONE

MAKES US

HOLY

Isaiah 43: 14 Thus saith the LORD, your redeemer, the *Holy One* of Israel...
Hebrews 12: 10 For our earthly fathers disciplined us for a few years, doing the best they knew how. But God's discipline is always right and good for us because it means we will share in his *holiness*. (NLT)

13

THE MAN OF SORROW

WANTS TO

WIPE AWAY YOUR TEARS

Isaiah 53: 3 He is despised and rejected of men; a *man of sorrows*, and acquainted with grief:
Isaiah 25: 8 The Sovereign Lord will wipe away all *tears.* (NLT)

Exodus 3: 14 And God said unto Moses, I AM THAT I AM: and he said, Thus shalt thou say unto the children of Israel, *I AM* hath sent me unto you.

TODAY

JESUS IS

OUR ADVOCATE

≫ ≫ ≫ ≫ ≫ ≫ ≫ ≫ ≫ ≫ ≫ ≫ ≫

TOMORROW

OUR JUDGE

1 John 2: 1 ...And if any man sin, we have an *advocate* with the Father, Jesus Christ the righteous:
2 Corinthians 5: 10 For we must all stand before Christ to be *judged*. We will each receive whatever we deserve for the good or evil we have done in our bodies. (NLT)

16

Section II

THE FAMILY

REPLACE EROS WITH

AGAPE

AND YOU WILL

REPLACE DIVORCE

WITH

ANNIVERSARIES

20th   40th   60th

Colossians 3: 18, 19 Wives submit yourselves unto your own husbands, as it is fit in the Lord. Husbands love your wives and be not bitter against them.

18

L O O S E N   U P

A LITTLE

AND TIGHTEN UP

YOUR FAMILY TIES

Proverbs 5: 18 ...rejoice with the wife of thy youth.
Proverbs 17: 22 A merry heart doeth good like a medicine: but a broken spirit drieth the bones.
Ephesians 6: 4 And, ye fathers, provoke not your children to wrath: but bring them up in the nurture and admonition of the Lord

LISTEN to your children

And they will

LISTEN to you

Proverbs 22: 6 Train up a child in the way he should go: and when he is old, he will not depart from it.

Discipline brings Correction

Provoking to anger brings Dissension

Proverbs 6: 23 The *correction of discipline* is the way to life.(NLT)
Colossians 3: 21 Fathers, *provoke not your children to anger*, least
they be discouraged.

21

THE SON

MAKES A HAPPY

Psalm 144: 15 Happy is that people... whose God is the Lord.

Know who you bee

And

bee it in Jesus

Acts 17: 28 For in Him we live and move and have our being.

OK,

FLOWER   CHILDREN

NOW IS   THE TIME
TO BLOOM   FOR JESUS

II Corinthians 6: 2 ...now is the accepted time; behold now is the day of salvation.

YOU WANT FREEDOM ?

BE DEBT FREE ... FROM CREDIT

AND DEBT FREE ... FROM SIN

Envy – strife – adultery
Bad thoughts – selfish – pride
Wild parties – gossip – anger
All listed in Gal 5:19-21

Matthew 6: 12 And forgive us our *debts* as we forgive our *debtors*.
Romans 13: 8 Owe no man anything but to love

GREED FOR THE WORD

brings   PROSPERITY.

GREED FOR MONEY

brings   CALAMITY.

Proverbs 15: 27 He that is *greedy of gain troubleth* his own house.
Matthew 6: 24,33 No man can serve two masters...Ye cannot serve
God and mammon. But seek ye first the Kingdom of God...and all
these things shall be added unto you.
I Chronicles 29: 12 Both riches and honor come of thee.

FISHERS OF MEN

NEVER

SMELL FISHY

Matthew 4: 19 Follow me, and I will make you *fishers of men*.

27

STOCK IN HEAVEN

NEVER DEPRECIATES.

YOU ARE GUARANTEED

A HEALTHY RETURN.

Matthew 6: 19-20 Lay not up...treasures upon earth, where moth and rust doth corrupt, and where thieves break thru and steal: But lay up for yourself treasures in heaven where neither moth nor rust doeth corrupt, and where thieves do not break through and steal.

Section III

THE STRESSED

INSTEAD OF THROWING

YOUR LIFE

AWAY,

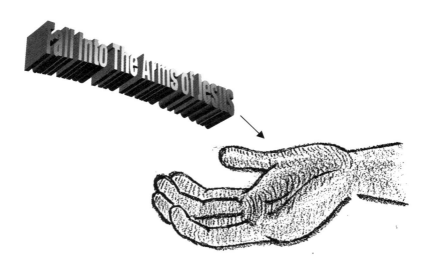

Deuteronomy 33: 27 The eternal God is thy refuge, and underneath are the everlasting arms: and He shall thrust out the enemy before thee;

HAVING   TR

OUBLE   COPING ?

LET JESUS COPE

WITH

YOUR   TROUBLES

WHEN YOU HAVE GOD –
YOU HAVE NO WORRIES.

Psalm 34: 6 This poor man cried, and the Lord heard him, and saved him out of all his troubles.

OH YE OF LITTLE FAITH

BECOME

OH YE OF HEAP BIG

PROBLEMS

Matthew 9: 28... and Jesus saith unto them, Believe ye that I am able to do this?

Matthew 14: 29-31... when Peter was come down out of the ship, he walked on the water, to go to Jesus. But when he saw the wind boisterous, he was afraid, and beginning to sink, he cried, saying, Lord, save me. And immediately Jesus stretched forth His hand and caught him, and said unto him, *O thou of little faith*, wherefore didst thou doubt?

DEAL WITH IT

Or

DROWN IN IT

Cares   Problems

Lust   Sin   Greed

I Timothy 6: 6, 9 ... godliness with contentment is great gain.
...they that will be rich fall into temptation and a snare, and into
many foolish and hurtful lusts, which *drown* men in destruction
and perdition.

33

Why Consider Suicide ?

Jesus Already Died

FOR YOU

I Thessalonians 5: 9, 10 For God hath not appointed us to wrath, but to obtain salvation by our Lord Jesus Christ, who *died for us;*

Tired of guiding your own tour

thru life ?

GOD IS THE BEST TOUR GUIDE EVER ... He has

been at it

since the beginning of time,

Psalm 48: 14 For this God is our God for ever and ever: He will be our guide even unto death.
Psalm 32: 8 I will instruct thee and teach thee in the way which thou shalt go: I will guide thee with mine eye.

YOU DECIDE*

DELIVERANCE ----

OR

DESTRUCTION

Psalm 32: 7 Thou art my hiding place; thou shalt preserve me from trouble; thou shalt compass me about with songs of *deliverance*.

Empty yourself

TO GOD

AND

Never be empty again.

Matthew 5: 6 Blessed are they which do hunger and thirst after righteousness: for they shall be filled.
Romans 15: 13 Now the God of hope fill you with all joy and peace...

THE MEAT OF THE

WILL MEET YOUR

John 4: 32, 34 But He said unto them, I have meat to eat that ye know not of. Jesus saith unto them, My meat is to do the will of Him that sent me, and to finish His work.

38

WHY OBEY MAN-MADE LAWS, BUT IGNORE GOD'S LAWS?

YOU WOULD ESCAPE JAIL, BUT END-UP IN HELL.

Romans 13: 2 So those who refuse to obey the laws of the land are refusing to obey God, and punishment will follow. (NLT)
Leviticus 18: 5 If you obey my laws and regulations, you will find life through them. I am the Lord. (NLT)

RUN TO JESUS ALL YE WHO ARE

WEARY

OR

RUN FROM HIM

AND

WORRY

Isaiah 28: 12 ...This is the rest wherewith ye may cause the weary to rest;...
Isaiah 40: 31 But they that wait upon the Lord shall renew their strength; they shall mount up with wings as eagles; they shall run, and not be *weary*; and they shall walk and not faint...

Section IV

THE CHURCH

God made

bees to produce

 honey,

He made

Christians to produce

 fruit.

Galatians 5: 22 But the fruit of the Spirit is love, joy, peace, longsuffering, gentleness, goodness, faith, meekness, temperance:

STRIVE

FOR

PERFECTION

ACCEPT

REDEMPTION

1 Kings 8: 61 Let your heart therefore be *perfect* with the Lord our God.
Ephesians 1 :7 In whom we have *redemption* through his blood, the forgiveness of sins;

43

Satisfy the flesh

and

Destroy your soul ....

.... Destroy the flesh

and

Satisfy your soul

Galatians 6: 8 For he that soweth to his flesh shall of the flesh reap corruption; but he that soweth to the Spirit shall of the Spirit reap life everlasting.
Luke 9: 24 For whosoever will save his life shall lose it: but whosoever will lose his life for my sake, the same shall save it.

Standing in the gap

WILL BUILD A BRIDGE

Ezekiel 22: 30 And I sought for a man among them, that should make up the hedge, and *stand in the gap* before me for the land, that I should not destroy it.

John 13: 34,35 ...Love one another as I have loved you...By this shall all men know that ye are my disciples.

LISTEN TO THE

STILL SMALL VOICE

TURN A DEAF EAR

TO A BOISTEROUS LIE

GOSSIP & LIES

God speaks to Elijah

I Kings 19: 11-13 ...Go forth and stand upon the mount before the LORD. And behold the LORD passed by, and a great and strong wind rent the mountains, and brake in pieces the rocks before the LORD, but the LORD was not in the wind, and after the wind an earthquake, but the LORD was not in the earthquake: After the earthquake a fire, but the LORD was not in the fire; and after the fire a *still small voice*. And it was so when Elijah heard it, that he wrapped his face in his mantle and went out...

47

Life is in the BLOOD

GOD GAVE EACH ONE OF US LIFE WITH A CERTAIN BLOOD TYPE.

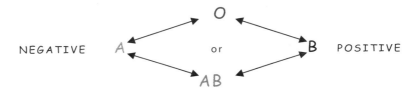

HE GIVES ETERNAL LIFE WITH ONLY ONE BLOOD TYPE ...

J

FOR JESUS

Leviticus 17: 11 For the life of the flesh is in the blood: and I have given it to you upon the altar to make an atonement for your souls:for it is the blood that maketh an atonement for the soul.

FATHER,

I COME BOLDLY TO
THE THRONE

AND BOW HUMBLY AT
JESUS' FEET

Hebrews 4: 16 Let us therefore come boldly unto the throne of grace, that we may obtain mercy, and find grace to help in time of need.
James 4: 10 Humble yourselves in the sight of the Lord, and he shall lift you up.

OPEN YOUR HEART
TO GOD

CLOSE YOUR MIND
TO EVIL

Psalm 119: 10 With my whole heart have I sought thee.
Psalm 34: 10 ...they that seek the LORD shall not want any good thing.
Proverbs 3: 7 ... fear the LORD and depart from evil.
Psalm 34:13 Keep thy tongue from evil;

LORD,

LET ME BE BLINDED

TO OTHERS' FAULTS

AND OPEN MINDED

TO MY OWN.

Matthew 7:3 ...why beholdest thou the mote that is in thy brother's eye, but considerest not the beam that is in thine own eye.

WE ALTER OUR CLOTHES
TO MAKE THEM FIT.

WE BOW AT THE ALTAR
TO MAKE US FIT.

Luke 9: 62 Jesus said unto him, No man, having put his hand to the plough, and looking back, is *fit* for the kingdom of God.

God made seasons

For a reason...

Reason what season

You are in

Ecclesiastes 3: 1 To everything there is a *season*, and a time to every purpose under the heaven.

WORK WHILE IT IS DAY

SLEEP THRU THE NIGHT

PRAY WITHOUT CEASING

John 9: 4 I must *work*...while it is day; the night cometh, when no man can work.
I Thessalonians 5: 17 Pray without ceasing.

54

RESCUE THE PERISHING

IF GOD HAS

RESCUED YOU FROM

PERISHING

John 10: 28 And I give unto them eternal life; and they shall never perish, neither shall any man pluck them out of my hand.
2 Peter 3: 9 The Lord is ... not willing that any should perish, but that all should come to repentance.
James 5: 19, 20 "Scripture taken from THE MESSAGE" If you know people who have wandered off from God's truth, don't Write them off, Go after them. Get them and you will have rescued precious lives from destruction. (TM)

Fruit that falls from our limbs

SHOULD BE RIPE

NOT ROTTEN

Galatians 5: 19--23 Now the *works of the flesh* are manifest, which are these; adultery, fornication, uncleanness, lasciviousness, idolatry, witchcraft, hatred, variance, emulations, wrath, strife, seditions, heresies, envyings, murders, drunkenness, revellings, and such like: of the which I tell you...that they which do such things shall not inherit the kingdom of God. But the *fruit of the Spirit* is love, joy, peace, longsuffering, gentleness, goodness, faith, meekness, temperance, against such there is no law.

WHY GOSSIP

WHEN YOU CAN WORSHIP?

Psalm 29: 2 Give unto the Lord the glory due unto his name; worship the Lord in the beauty of holiness.
Proverbs 11: 13 A gossip goes around revealing secrets, but those who are trustworthy can keep a confidence. (NLT)

LOVE THE

SINNER;

DESPISE HIS

SIN.

Leviticus 19: 18 ...Love thy neighbor as thyself.
Romans 6: 23 The wages of sin is death;

Section V

FOR ENCOURAGEMENT

Consumer's Choice

- ◆ BLESSINGS OR CURSES
- ◆ HEAVEN OR HELL
- ◆ LIFE OR DEATH
- ◆ GOOD OR EVIL
- ◆ OBEDIENCE OR DISOBEDIENCE
- ◆ HAPPINESS OR GNASHING OF TEETH

Deuteronomy 30: 15, 19 ...I have set before thee this day *life and good* and death *and evil*.
I have set before you...*blessing and cursing:*
Matthew 8:12 ...there shall be weeping and *gnashing of teeth*.

CAST YOUR BURDEN
ON THE LORD

AND LOSE WEIGHT

II Corinthians 5: 4 For we that are in this tabernacle (our bodies) do groan, being *burdened*...
Psalm 55: 22 *Cast thy burden upon the Lord*, and He shall sustain thee...

JUMP

FOR   JOY.

JOY

IS YOUR   STRENGTH.

Laughter - Happiness

Nehemiah 8: 10 ...neither be ye sorry, for the *joy* of the Lord is your *strength*.

YOU'RE IN GOOD HANDS

WITH THE ALMIGHTY

Psalm 91: 11, 12 For He shall give his angels charge over you to keep you in all your ways. They shall bear you up in their hands...
Deuteronomy 33: 3 Indeed, you love the people; all your holy ones are *in your hands...* (NLT)

63

IF YOU LIKE

♦ SCRATCH AND SNIFF

♦ ASK AND RECEIVE

Hidden Mysteries

♦ SEEK AND FIND

♦ KNOCK AND OPEN

Matthew 7: 7 Ask, and it shall be given you; seek, and ye shall find, knock, and it shall be opened unto you.

WHOEVER SAID "NOTHING IN LIFE IS FREE"

NEEDS TO MEET my

Jesus

blessings . honor . glory . power . riches . strength . wisdom

Romans 8: 32 He that spared not His own Son, but delivered Him up for us all, how shall He not with Him also *freely give* us all things.

COPY THE SCRIPTURE

PASTE IT IN YOUR HEART

CUT SIN

PASTE IT IN THE BLOOD

SAVE AS

C:/LAMBS BOOK OF LIFE/_____

Your Name

Psalm 119: 11 Thy word have I hid in mine heart, that I might not sin against thee.
Philippians 4: 3 ...those...whose names are in the book of life.
Revelation 3: 5 He that overcometh, the same shall be clothed in white raiment; and I will not blot out his name out of the book of life, but I will confess his name before my Father, and before his angels.

Psalm 1: 1 Blessed is the man that walketh not in the counsel of the ungodly...
Revelation 12: 10, 11 ...the accuser of our brethren is cast down, which accused them day and night. And they overcame him by the blood of the Lamb, and by the word of their testimony; and they loved not their lives unto death.

67

THE POT OF GOLD

AT THE END OF
THE RAINBOW

IS HEAVEN'S   THRONE

Revelations 4: 2, 3 ...a throne was set in heaven, and one sat on the throne. And he that sat was to look upon like a jasper and a sardine stone: and there was a rainbow around about the throne, in sight like unto an emerald.

SMILE a while

and give

YOUR FACE A REST...

REST a while

and give

YOUR FACE A LIFT

Isaiah 32: 18 And my people shall dwell in a peaceable habitation, and in sure dwellings, and in quiet resting places,...

Rainbow

...GOD'S COVENANT NOT TO DESTROY ALL FLESH

BY FLOOD

Cross

...GOD'S COVENANT NOT TO DESTROY ALL FLESH

BY FIRE

Genesis 9: 14, 15 It shall come to pass, when I bring a cloud over the earth, that the bow shall be seen in the cloud: And I will remember my covenant, which is between me and you and every living creature of all flesh; and the waters shall no more become a flood to destroy all flesh.

Luke 22: 20 After supper he took another cup of wine and said, "This wine is the token of God's new covenant to save you—an agreement sealed with the blood I will pour out for you. (NLT)

TO BE   OR NOT   TO BE

A CHRISTIAN

I CAN BE...

WILL I BE ?

YOU CAN BE...

WILL YOU BE ?

WE CAN BE...

WILL WE BE ?

THAT IS THE

Acts 26: 28 Agrippa said unto Paul, almost thou persuadest me to be a Christian. ...Paul said, I would...that thou were both almost and altogether.

 INSIDE

 OUTSIDE

UPSIDE

DOWNSIDE

I WANT THE HAPPY SIDE

GOD'S SIDE

Psalm 146: 5 Happy is he that hath the God of Jacob for his help, whose hope is in the Lord his God.

.

Section VI

FOR SALVATION

LOOKING FOR LOVE ?

FIND GOD

I John 4: 8 ...God is Love.

V IT OUT   LET JESUS IN

HE'LL CHANGE YOUR ROUTE AND CLEANSE YOU

FROM SIN

Psalm 51: 2 Wash me thoroughly from mine iniquity, and cleanse me from my sin.

AFTER JESUS

THERE IS LIFE

John 3: 16   For God so loved the world, that He gave His only begotten Son, that whosever believeth in Him should not perish, but have *everlasting life*.

PLAN NOW FOR YOUR TRIP INTO OUTER SPACE

DON'T DELAY

Make Your Reservations:

✝ CONFESS JESUS WITH YOUR MOUTH

✝ BELIEVE GOD RAISED HIM FROM THE DEAD

✝ REPENT OF YOUR SINS

✝ TURN FROM YOUR WICKED WAYS

ARRIVE AT YOUR DESTINATION IN THE
TWINKLING OF AN EYE

I Thessalonians 4: 16, 17 For the Lord Himself shall descend from heaven with a shout with the voice of the archangel and with the trump of God: and the dead in Christ shall rise first: Then we which are alive and remain shall be caught up together with them in the air, and so shall we ever be with the Lord.
I Corinthians 15: 51, 52 Behold, I shew you a mystery, We shall not all sleep, but we shall all be changed. In a moment, in the twinkling of an eye at the last trump: for the trumpet shall sound and the dead shall be raised...

Y
O
U

W
I
N

SELL OUT TO GOD...

Y
O
U

L
O
S
E

SELL OUT   TO SATAN...

Mark 10: 21 ... Then Jesus said...go thy way, sell whatsoever thou hast, and give to the poor, and thou shalt have treasure in heaven: *Matthew 26: 14, 15* ...Judas Iscariot, went unto the chief priests, and said unto them, what will ye give me, and I will deliver Him unto you? And they convenated with him for thirty pieces of silver. *Matthew 27: 5* ...and he cast down the pieces of silver; ... and departed and went and hanged himself.

DIE TO FLESH

BURNING DESIRES

BE BORN OF THE SPIRIT

I Peter 3: 18 For Christ also hath once suffered for sins, the just for the unjust, that he might bring us to God, being put to death in the flesh, but quickened by the Spirit.
Romans 8: 13 For if ye live after the flesh, ye shall die: but if ye through the Spirit do mortify the deeds of the body, ye shall live.

79

TIRED OF LIVING ALONE ???

☺ I WOULD LOVE TO LIVE WITH YOU

☺ I WILL TRULY UNDERSTAND YOU

☺ I WILL NOT MAKE A MESS FOR YOU TO CLEAN UP... I CAN HELP CLEAN UP YOUR MESSES

☺ I WILL NOT EAT YOUR FOOD...INSTEAD, I WILL GIVE YOU MEAT TO EAT THAT YOU KNOW NOT OF

☺ I WILL NOT BE A BURDEN TO YOU...I WILL SHARE YOUR BURDENS

☺ YOUR EMOTIONS ARE IMPORTANT TO ME

☺ TALK...I WILL LISTEN

☺ GIVE ME A CHANCE, YOU MIGHT LIKE IT

JESUS

Matthew 28: 20 ...lo, I am with you alway, even unto the end of the world. Amen.

YOU ARE THE GUARANTEED WINNER

OF THE

GRAND PRIZE

✡ A MULTI-MILLION DOLLAR HOME

✡ STREETS OF PURE GOLD

✡ RIVER OF LIFE FLOWS CLOSE BY

✡ TREE OF LIFE IN NEARBY GARDEN

✡ LOCATED IN MUCH DESIRED CITY

IF YOU HAVE MET THE REQUIREMENTS LISTED ON THE FOLLOWING PAGE

You will find a complete description of this city in the book of Revelation, chapters 21 and 22.

Have you prayed this prayer?

Dear God,

Your Word says, "If I will confess with my mouth the Lord Jesus, and shall believe in my heart that God has raised Him from the dead, I shall be saved." (Rom. 10:9)

I believe that Jesus is my Lord. I confess Him as my Master, my Savior, and my Lord. I receive Him now into my heart by faith.

Thank you, Jesus, for suffering my penalty on the cross. You paid the full price for my redemption. I believe that God forgives me now, as your blood washes away my sin. I know I am forgiven. I am, now, God's child.

Thank You, Lord!

JESUS IS THE ONLY WAY TO GOD. IF YOU ACCEPT HIM AS YOUR SAVIOR, THEN GOD WILL WRITE YOUR NAME IN THE LAMB'S BOOK OF LIFE, WHICH ENTITLES YOU TO THE GRAND PRIZE -- ETERNAL LIFE.

Revelation 21: 7, 8 All who are victorious will inherit all these blessings, and I will be their God, and they will be my children. But cowards who turn away from me, and unbelievers, and the corrupt, and murderers, and the immoral, and those who practice witchcraft, and idol worshipers, and all liars-their doom is in the lake that burns with fire and sulfur. This is the second death. (NLT)

Bad Credit ???

Salvation Is Free !!

Romans 3: 24 Being justified freely by His grace through the redemption that is in Christ Jesus.

Pardon Me

Have Your Sins

Been Pardoned?

Psalm 34: 22 But the Lord will redeem those who serve him. Everyone who trusts in him will be freely pardoned. (NLT)

84

Section VII

THE OMEGA

Satan has many ways

TO HELL

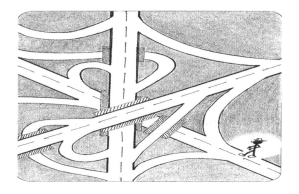

JESUS IS THE ONLY WAY

TO HEAVEN!

John 14: 6 Jesus saith unto him, I am the way, the truth, and the life: no man cometh unto the Father, but by me.
Proverbs 14: 12 There is a way which seemeth right unto a man, but the end thereof are the ways of death.

LET THE
LIGHT OF THE WORLD

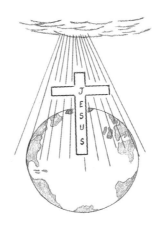

LEAD YOU
OUT OF DARKNESS

John 8: 12 Jesus said to the people, "I am the light of the world. If you follow me, you won't be stumbling through the darkness, because you will have the light that leads to life." (NLT)

THE SON OF MAN

IS THE

SON OF GOD

\

Matthew 20: 28 For even I, the Son of Man, came here not to be served   but to serve others, and to give my life as a ransom for many. (NLT)

STOP AIMLESSLY

DRIFTING;

ANCHOR IN THE ROCK···

JESUS!

I Corinthians 10: 4 And did all drink the same spiritual drink: for they drank of that spiritual Rock that followed them: and that Rock was Christ.

Hebrews 6: 18, 19 ...Therefore we who have fled to him for refuge can take new courage, for we can hold on to his promise with confidence. This confidence is like a strong and trustworthy anchor for our souls. It leads us through the curtain of heaven into God's inner sanctuary. (NLT)

LET THE PRINCE OF PEACE

CALM YOUR STORM

Isaiah 26: 3 Thou wilt keep him in perfect peace, whose mind is stayed on thee:

Isaiah 9: 6 For unto us a child is born, unto us a son is given: and the government shall be upon his shoulder: and his name shall be called ... The Prince of Peace

Mark 4: 39 And he arose, and rebuked the wind, and said unto the sea, Peace, be still.   And the wind ceased, and there was a great calm.

WILL NOT

HARBOR GOATS

John 10: 14 I am the *good shepherd*; I know my own sheep, and they know me, (NLT)
Matthew 25: 32, 33 And before him shall be gathered all nations: and he shall separate them one from another, as a shepherd divideth his sheep from the goats:And he shall set the sheep on his right hand, but the goats on the left.

91

JESUS OFFERS LIVING WATER;

SATAN OFFERS DRIED-UP SPRINGS.

John 4: 10   Jesus replied, "If you only knew the gift God has for you and who I am, you would ask me, and I would give you *living water.* (NLT)
2 Peter 2: 17, 18   These people are as useless as *dried-up springs of water* or as clouds blown away by the wind-promising much and delivering nothing. They are doomed to blackest darkness. They brag about themselves with empty, foolish boasting. With lustful desire as their bait, they lure back into sin   those who have just escaped from such wicked living. (NLT)

THE ALPHA AND OMEGA

IS OUR

AUTHOR & FINISHER.

Revelation 22: 13 I am *Alpha and Omega*, the beginning and the end, the first and the last.
Hebrews 12: 2 Looking unto Jesus the *author and finisher* of our faith;